Maybole: Past And Present

Roderick Lawson

Maybole

Past and Present.

BY

REV. R. LAWSON,

AUTHOR OF "CROSSRAGUEL ABBEY," ETC.

J. AND R. PARLANE,

PAISLEY.

1885.

PREFATORY NOTE.

This little book is written for my fellow townsmen, as a contribution towards the better knowledge of the history of our town. The facts which it contains have been gathered from many sources; but as I have taken some pains to verify them, I think their accuracy may be generally depended on. Maybole may appear common-place to others, but to those whose life's history has been connected with it, the old town must ever be surrounded by a halo. There have been tragedies and comedies here as elsewhere, and the history of a town is but as the history of the world at large. I trust that natives of Maybole, who are scattered abroad, may be pleased to have a memento of the place of their birth, as calculated to foster a local attachment which should in no wise be lost sight of. I have striven to write it in as interesting a way as I could, and, with the help of friends, have sought to lighten its pages with some neat engravings. Perhaps I have introduced too many verses, but it is hoped that these will be pardoned on account of their local character. It is not written either for fame or profit, but simply as a means of possible usefulness, and a desire to do a little for the credit of the town. Everybody should take an interest in the place where his lot is cast; and one of my aims will be served if it help to stir up in us a feeling of patriotism, and a laudable desire to promote, in all ways open to us, the well-being of the "little city of our dwelling which we belong to on this side the grave." And my highest aim will be attained, if the book help in any wise to teach the sacredness of home, as the spot where our life-tragedy has been appointed us, and which must therefore ever have an interest to us over all other places.

R. L.

CONTENTS.

ILLUSTRATIONS.

THE KINGDOM OF CARRICK.

Among the bonny windin' banks,
Where Doon rins, wimplin', clear,
Where Bruce ance ruled the martial ranks,
And shook his Carrick spear.

WHEN the traveller by the Glasgow and South-Western Railway passes the town of Ayr, and crosses the river Doon, he finds himself in a district differing considerably in physical features from that in which he has hitherto been journeying. The somewhat flat monotony of central Ayrshire is broken up, and a more picturesque region makes its appearance. Mochrum and the ridge of Brown Carrick hill start from the sea-shore, the fine range of the Straiton hills bound the prospect on the east, while away to the south there rise a confused tangle of swelling green summits stretching on to far-off Loch Ryan.

This district of Ayrshire, comprising all south of the Doon, is the ancient "kingdom of Carrick," famous of old for its hardy race of fighting men. This quality was fostered in early days by the genius of Bruce, and the tastes of the "fighting Kennedys," who ruled the district after the Bruces. And this fact of their fighting pre-eminence has been handed down in an old adage, of unknown antiquity, which thus characterises what an Englishman would call the "ridings" of Ayrshire, as well as the neighbouring district to the south:

Carrick for a man,
  Kyle for coo,
Cunningham for butter and cheese,
  Galloway for woo.*

The fact of Galloway being here brought in along with the three divisions of Ayrshire, points to the circumstance that in ancient times these were generally classed together. In fact, Carrick, when first known in history, was owned by the same family who ruled in Galloway. This family is generally known under the name of the Macdowalls, although a friend, versed in these matters, assures me that "Duncan, Earl of Carrick, the founder of the Ayrshire branch, was not a Macdowall. His name was simply 'Duncan, son of Gilbert,' or 'Duncan of Carrick.' The Macdowalls of Galloway are supposed in some way to be connected with these old lords of Galloway, but how, no one knows, as there are no early charters existing."

But whatever their surname was, or whether they had a surname at all, does not matter much, as the family soon received a new one, dear to every Scottish heart. For in 1271, Marjory, Countess of Carrick, was married to Robert Bruce, Earl of Annandale; and from their union sprang the great king Robert. Whether the founder of Scottish in-

* It is quite true that the folks of central Ayrshire persist in reading the old lines, "Kyle for a man," &c., but this is mere local prejudice! Even the very rhythm of the lines, if there were nothing else, might teach them the true reading.

dependence was born at Turnberry or at Lochmaben, has been disputed, in absence of any authentic records. But from the fact of Turnberry being the maternal residence (and probably the larger residence of the two), as well as from the peculiar circumstances attending the marriage—it being a sort of run-away one—*she* running away with *him!*—it is stoutly held by all Ayrshire folk that the hero of Bannockburn was an Ayrshire man, and born in the kingdom of Carrick. Sir Walter Scott was evidently of this opinion when he makes Bruce say, at the capture of Turnberry, in the "Lord of the Isles":

"For now once more my sire's abode
Is mine—behold the floor I trod
In tottering infancy!
And there the vaulted arch, whose sound
Echoed my joyous shout and bound
In boyhood, and that rung around
To youth's unthinking glee!"

At Bannockburn, too, the men of Carrick formed part of the division under Bruce's own special command,

"Reserved for aid where needed most."

And at the crisis of the battle, when the king brought up this reserve, we may see what trust he placed in the bravery of his native district:

"I, with my Carrick spearmen, charge,
Now, forward to the shock!"
At once the spears were forward thrown,
Against the sun the broad-swords shone;
The pibroch lent its maddening tone,
And loud King Robert's voice was known—
"Carrick, press on!—they fail, they fail—
Press on, brave sons of Innisfail,
The foe is fainting fast!"

In almost every battle fought in Scotland we find men of Carrick present. At Largs, Bannockburn, Flodden Field, Solway Moss, Langside, Bothwell Bridge—we find Kennedys, Cathcarts, and Boyds, giving and receiving blows, and coming in for a more than ordinary share of wounds and "glory." And not content with fighting in their own country, some of them went over to the Continent and engaged in the wars there; and we read of Hew Kennedy of Bargany, in 1421, defending the Bridge of Beaux, in Anjou, with one hundred soldiers, in such gallant fashion that he received "great reward of the king," and came home a famous man.

In these modern times, the old kingdom of Carrick has been divided into nine parishes, which rank according to population, in the following order:—

Maybole,	6,622	Town, 4,474
Girvan,	5,476	Town, 4,501
Dailly,	2,204	
Colmonell,	2,191	
Kirkmichael,	1,989	
Kirkoswald,	1,776	
Ballantrae,	1,440	
Straiton,	1,240	
Barr,	600	

It is of Maybole, as the recognised "capital" of this "kingdom," that I here purpose to give some account.

Crossraguel Abbey.

HOW MAYBOLE AROSE.

Minibole's a dirty hole,
It sits abune a mire.

The first point of interest about a town is its name; and our one, I am proud to say, is a respectable one. It is so ancient that nobody with certainty knows the meaning of it. The oldest form of the name apparently is *Meybothel*—the way it is spelled in the charter of the Parish Church in 1193. This form of the word, however, only occurs once. The next form it assumed was *Miniboll*—the way it is spelled by the Rev. William Abercrummie in 1686. In the old Town Council Records it is invariably spelled *Mayboill*, until about a hundred years ago, when it was changed into *Maybole*.

As to what Maybole means, etymologists differ. *Maigh* in Gaelic means a field or plain, and *buile* means a fold for cows; so that it might mean *the plain of the fold*, although that is rather prosaic. Or again, *boile* means strife, so that Maybole may mean *the field of strife;* which is much more romantic, and more likely too. My own opinion inclines to Minibole as the original form, seeing there are so many other *Minis* here about; and *Mini* in Gaelic means a marsh. As to *bole*, my opinion is that it is one of the many forms of *Bal*, a town; so that Minibole would mean *the town by the marsh*, which it plainly would be in days before what we call "the Bog" was drained and turned into arable land.

Be the etymology what it may, however, the name itself in its modern form is one of which any town may well feel proud. What a fine, mouth-filling sound it has! There is no name of a town along the whole line of the Glasgow and South-Western Railway which is for a moment to be compared with it. Ayr, for instance, is plainly too short, and Kilmarnock too long. Troon and Beith are insignificant. Girvan and Greenock want sound, and Paisley wants strength. Kilwinning is too smooth, and Ardrossan too rough. Even Glasgow is no better than it should be. But Maybole is simply perfect. It could not be improved upon. It is just the proper length, and contains the due proportion of vowels and consonants. Nature evidently designed it as the name of a place of note, and of something superior to the common run! *

*I confess, however, that my pride received a somewhat severe shock on hearing the name of our good town pronounced in London-English as *My-bowl!*

By degrees the little *clachan by the marsh* grew in size. But it had no church. The good Duncan, first Earl of Carrick, who lived at Turnberry, and who afterward founded the Abbey of Crossraguel, saw and pitied our forlorn condition, and built a Parish Church for us. This was in 1193. In that year Earl Dunçan, in the pious phraseology of the period, "gifted to God and Saint Mary of Melrose, the haill lands of Meybothel and Beltoc" as a permanent endowment for a parish church. Here, then, Maybole is fairly placed on its feet as an independent parish. It has now a church of its own, dedicated to St. Cuthbert, and a "God's Acre" round it, where our forefathers might lay their bones at death in hallowed ground. For it need hardly be said that the church first planted at the foot of the Kirk Wynd would be a Roman Catholic Church, and the churchyard round it would be consecrated, so far at least as that could be done by human hands.

But this Parish Church, founded by Duncan of Turnberry, was very small, and the little village was growing; so another benefactor arose in the person of Sir John Kennedy, of Dunure, ancestor of the present Marquess of Ailsa, who in 1371 built and endowed a second church for us, which exists to the present day. This is the Collegiate Church of Maybole, familiarly known among us as the *Auld College.* This name has nothing to do with what *we* call a College or place of learning; but it denotes a church which has a college or corporation of priests, and a daily service of public worship like a cathedral. Our Maybole Collegiate Church has the distinction of having been one of the first of its kind in Scotland. It had a Provost or Principal, and three prebends, was dedicated to the Virgin Mary, and survived till the period of the Reformation. It was in the house of the Rev. Andrew Gray, Provost of this church, that the famous debate with John Knox took place. The most of the ground on which the town now stands at one time belonged to it; and Lord Ailsa owes his dignity of *Superior* of Maybole to the fact of his being heir-at-law to the provost and prebendaries of the collegiate church. The charter gifting the church declares that it was founded for the purpose of celebrating daily divine service, "for the happy state of Sir John Kennedy, his wife Mary, and their children."

In this way, then, our town began to grow in size and respectability, as well, doubtless, as in intelligence and piety. What a boon it would have been to us, had any of these priests in those old days thought of writing a sketch of the past history and present condition of their town! But no age or place seems interesting to those who live in it.. It is only when many years have passed, and we look at it through the misty veil of antiquity, that we long to be able to realise the days that are no more.

The etymology of a few of our local names may be here inserted: *Dailly*, the dale or valley. *Straiton*, the town in the strath or plain. *Mochrum*, the ridge of the swine. *Cairnsmore*, the big cairn. *Bennan*, the little hill. *Craigfin*, the fair hill. *Craigdow*, the black hill. *Craigengower*, the hill of the goats. *Ailsa*, the rocky isle. *Auchendrane*, the field of the thorn. *Kilkerran*, the cell of St. Kiaran. *Ayr*, the clear river. *Doon*, the black river. *Girvan*, the rough river.

Old Market Cross, Edinburgh.

THE CHARTER AND TOWN RECORDS.

Dun-Edin's cross, a pillar'd stone,
Rose on a turret octagon;
But now is razed that monument,
    Whence royal edict rang.
And voice of Scotland's law was sent
    In glorious trumpet-clang.*

The Market Cross of Maybole formerly stood in the centre of High Street, nearly opposite the present Post Office. In the Castle Garden there are two stones which once formed part of it. One of these has the well-known

* Most readers of this will be aware that Mr Gladstone has recently re-erected the Cross of Edinburgh in all its ancient splendour.

three cross-crosslets of the Kennedy arms; while the other evidently served as a sun-dial. In the Council Records there is the following minute regarding it:—"Oct. 6, 1773.—The magistrates having taken under their consideration that the Cross of Mayboill as it stands at present is ane obstruction and hinderance to coaches and carridges as they pass and repass along the street, therefore, they unanimously agree and are of opinion that the same should be taken away, and that in place thereof there should be laid a Cross of Freestone, equal with the pavement, within a circle, neatly paved with small pebbles of whinstone, which they affirm and ordain to be the Cross of the Burgh of Mayboill in all time hereafter." This neatly paved Cross of Freestone has, however, disappeared, leaving only the present unmeaning square of causeway stones to mark the spot. Round the Market Cross in former days all the goods offered for sale were arranged, and it was from its steps that all legal proclamations were made.

The Market Cross introduces two important documents in the history of our town, of which notice must now be taken. The first of these is the Town Charter, a curious old document written in Latin and dated 14th Nov., 1516. It was given under the hand of James V., or rather of his guardian, John, Duke of Albany; for at that time James was but a child, and his father, James IV., had fallen three years before at Flodden. It begins by saying that the Charter was granted by the king for the special favour he bore "towards our beloved cousin and counsellor, Gilbert, Earl of Cassillis, and our devout priests, the provost and prebendaries of the collegiate church of Maybole." This Gilbert was the second Earl of Cassillis, and father of Abbot Quintin who debated with John Knox. He was afterwards killed at Prestwick, near Ayr, 1527, by Hugh Campbell of Loudon, sheriff of Ayr.

The Charter goes on to grant to the inhabitants of Maybole "full power and free faculty of buying and selling within the same, wine, wax, woollen and linen cloth (both broad and narrow), and all other merchandise; and with power and liberty of having and holding in the said burgh, bakers, brewers, fleshers, and vendors as well of flesh as of fish, and all other tradesmen belonging to a free burgh of barony." The charter grants likewise, "that there be in the said burgh free burgesses, and that they have power, in all time to come, of electing annually bailies, and all other officers necessary for the government of the said burgh, with power to the burgesses and inhabitants of the said burgh of having and holding therein a *Market Cross* for ever, and a market upon Thursdays every week, and Public Fairs yearly, at the Feast of the Bondage of St. Peter, viz., Lammas day, and for eight days following, with all tolls and liberties pertaining to Public Fairs, or that justly thereto may pertain in any manner of way."

Such is our Charter; and it may be noticed that it is of a somewhat superior style to that of common burghs of barony. In fact, it comes very near to the style of a royal burgh, like Ayr, and classes us among burghs of regality, which lifts our head up a bit. The days of burgh privileges are now past, however, and the duties of the Town Council are mainly in the hands of the Police Commissioners; but at one time these privileges were highly valued, and doubtless contributed to our prosperity. So highly were they valued, that two law pleas were waged over them. One of these was by a reforming party in the town in 1820, who wished to claim for the burgesses power to elect the bailies by popular vote, as was seemingly granted by the charter; but this was defeated. The other was by the Earl of Cassillis, about the same time, who wished to have it decreed that he had the sole right, as superior of the ground on which the greater part of the town stood, to appoint the bailies himself. But this at last seems to have been departed from, so that Maybole Town Council defeated both reformers and anti-reformers, and went on its way rejoicing.

The other document I have referred to is the Book of the Town Council Records, a volume of portentous size. It does not go further back, however, than December 23, 1721; the previous books having been either lost or destroyed. The book opens with a list of the Acts and Statutes of the Magistrates and Councillors; some of which are quaint enough. For instance: it is statuted and ordained that no person shall presume to wash any foul clothes, fishes, or entrails of beasts, in the well called St. Cuthbert's well, or in the current strain that runs therefrom betwixt the said well and that house called Abbot's Place, under the penalty of 22 shillings Scots money. It is likewise statuted and ordained that none of the inhabitants shall set any houses to idle or infamous persons that have no trades to live by, except by the advice of the bailies of the burgh; nor lodge or entertain in their houses sturdy and idle beggars or vagabonds, or sell them meat or drink, under the penalty of five pounds Scots. It is likewise statuted and ordained that none of the inhabitants shall presume to buy more cheese or leather in the market than will stock themselves, until the town be served; that fleshers shall be obliged to make sale of what beef or mutton they shall have in their booths in haills or in quarters, or in shares, so that those who have not use for the haill carcase may have a quarter or a share; that no baker shall refuse to bake in his oven for any of the inhabitants their meal or flour, he being at home; and that all goods exposed for sale on market-days shall be visited by persons appointed by the magistrates, and in case they find any insufficient saddles, shoes, &c., they shall report the same to the magistrates, that they may be punished. Finally, a warning is held out to any person who shall draw his stack without previously acquainting some two of his neighbours, or who shall go through his neighbour's yard without liberty asked and given, or who shall refuse to turn out with his horse and cart and carry the military baggage when warned by the magistrates—that in future, such things cannot be allowed in this well-governed community, but will be visited by certain fines in Scots money.

Elsewhere, throughout this volume of Council Records, there is not much of general interest. There is a good deal said about custom dues collected by an official called the *Customer*; and there is still more said about burgesses, "admitted, created, and received for good deeds done, and to be done by them to the said town," and who must all be certified as good and loyal subjects of His Majesty. The burgess fee was a guinea to strangers, and ten shillings to those whose fathers had been burgesses before them; and a burgess ticket was indispensable to all wishing to trade in the town.

On 14th February, 1797, it was resolved to offer a corps of volunteers "from the respectable inhabitants of the burgh and neighbourhood, to consist of 114 men, and to be called the Loyal Carrick Volunteers, the Earl of Cassillis to take command." And not content with providing volunteers, the magistrates in the following year ordained a general subscription in aid of the Government, "at this critical period, when the nation is threatened with the invasion of an enemy, whose aim is the destruction of our religion, our laws, and our liberty." I was curious to know how much the town gave to such a purpose, but though I searched diligently, I could not find it; I fear the Government was not much the richer by it. But it showed at least the spirit of the country at the time, and how hard it was faring at headquarters during the great French wars, when Maybole had thus to stand up and pat the back of the British Lion! In the possession of one of our townspeople, there is a list of seventy-seven of our inhabitants who set down their names with others in the "County of Air" in that old time, to serve as volunteers if called on; and the manner in which they are scheduled is curious: "Horse—armed with swords, pistols; Foot—armed with firelocks, pikes; Labourers with felling axes, pickaxes, spades, shovels, bere-hooks, saws; Cattle-herds; Carters; Riflemen." I have seen also a subscription sheet "for the purpose of treating the Cameronians, or 26th Regiment of foot, on their march through Maybole to Ireland, with a glass of spirits and a bake*, on the 2nd, 4th, 5th, and 6th days of December, 1803; who did, as is handed down by tradition, originate in this parish in the reign of James II." The Cameronian Regiment "originated" on Douglas Moor in the spring of 1689; but it is traditionally reported that the first man who enlisted was a man from Knockbrake in our neighbourhood. It may also be mentioned, that a little beyond the 1½ milestone, near Slateford, there is an old "Scotch" milestone, which formed the rallying place for the youths of Maybole to meet the soldiers on their march from Ayr, and escort them through the town.

* Account rendered :—6¼ gallons whiskie, £2 · 6 · 9; loaves and bakes, £0 · 10 · 10; balance to the poor, £0 · 15 · 11; total, £3 · 13 · 6.

St. Salvator's College, St. Andrews
(founded by Bishop Kennedy).

THE STORY OF THE KENNEDYS.

'Twixt Wigtown and the toon o' Ayr,
And laigh doon by the cruives o' Cree;
Nae man shall get a lodging there,
Unless he court wi' Kennedy.

But I am weary to get away from these old musty documents down among the press of men, for our history is a stirring history, and has scenes in it which may well claim the pen of the poet or the novelist. When, therefore, we turn from legal records to the page of the historian, we find ourselves in a very different region indeed. We find ourselves here in the midst of a wild and turbulent district, owned by a number of brawling chiefs, many of whose fortresses remain in ruined grandeur until this day. One peculiarity of these chiefs was, that they were nearly all related to each other, and nearly all of the name of Kennedy. Kennedy, in fact, is a name indigenous to Carrick. There were Kennedys of Dunure, of Bargany, of Garryhorn, of Blairquhan, of Baltersan, of Girvan Mains. The exception was, when the name was not Kennedy; as, for example, when it was Boyd or Cathcart. In the vast majority of cases, the land was owned and the fields tilled by the great Carrick clan—Kennedy.

Chief of all the Kennedys were the Dunure Kennedys, a family which, beginning first as simple Lairds of Dunure, gradually became Lords Kennedy, Earls of Cassillis, and finally Marquesses of Ailsa. They were a clever, brave, but somewhat unscrupulous race of men, these Dunure Kennedys, with no end of ambition in them, and ever on the outlook for more land and more power. They were wonderfully prudent, too, with all their rapacity. They always knew how far to go with safety. And even when they did stretch a point, as when they roasted Allan Stewart of Crossraguel, or killed poor Bargany on his road from Ayr, they knew how to make friends at Court, so that they might not rouse too much the ire of the Sovereign. They were always kindly towards Maybole too, which ought to go for something with us; and the terror inspired by their name made our town secure in days when security was the first condition of prosperity.

And, then, there is a dash of gallantry about some of them which one likes to read of. One, for instance, called Alexander *Dalgour*, or Alexander of the Dagger, had done something to offend the mighty Earl of Wigtown of those times. The earl offered a reward of the forty Mark lands of Stewarton to any one who should bring him Alexander's head. A happy thought strikes the *Dalgour*. "Why not carry my own head to him myself and claim the reward?" No sooner said than done. He gathered a company of 100 horsemen, and came to the town of Wigtown on Christmas morning, about the time he knew the earl would be at church. Having previously got a deed drawn up in due form assigning him the lands of Stewarton, he marched into the church at the head of his followers, and thus addressed the astonished earl: "My lord, you have offered this forty Mark land to any that would bring you my head, and I know there is none so meet as myself. And therefore I will desire your lordship to keep to me as you would to any other." The earl perceived that if he refused, it might cost him his life, and so he took the pen and subscribed the same. Alexander thanked his lordship, and, taking his horse, "lap on and cam his ways." This story, it must be confessed, looks a little fabulous; but there are grounds for believing it to be substantially correct.

Another celebrated Kennedy of a different stamp was James Kennedy, Bishop of St. Andrews, and at one time Chancellor of Scotland. He flourished during the minority of James III., and founded the College of St. Salvator's at St. Andrews in 1450. He was regarded as the greatest and best man of his age, and his death was lamented by all good men as though they had lost a public father. He assigned a large sum of money to build a tomb for himself in St. Andrews, which still remains; a monument of his wealth, and also of a weakness, from which, with all his virtues, he was not exempt. Lindsay says of him, "he founded a triumphant college at St. Andrews, called St. Salvator's College, wherein he made his *lair* very curiously and costly; and also, he bigged a ship called the Bishop's Berge; and when all three were complete, he knew not which of the three was costliest."

David, first Earl of Cassillis, was slain at the battle of Flodden Field. Gilbert, the second earl, was the one who obtained the Town Charter for us. Gilbert, the third earl, was a man of note in the Scottish politics of his day, and was supposed to have been poisoned in France for opposing the wishes of the French court. Gilbert, the fourth earl, was "ane werry greidy manne" according to the ancient historian, "wha cairitt nocht how he gatt land, sa that he culd cum be the samin." It was he who roasted Commendator Stewart in the Black Vault of Dunure. He fought also for Queen Mary at Langside. It was John, the fifth earl, who killed young Bargany, near the Lady Cross, 11th December, 1601, on that cold wintry day when the snow fell so thick that you "culd not see the lenthe of ane lanse befoir you." John, the sixth earl, was a better specimen. He was a leader among the Presbyterians, and was one of the three ruling elders sent up to the Westminster Assembly of 1643. He is known as the "grave and solemn earl;" and it was his lady, according to the old tradition, who ran off with the "gypsy laddie."

As to the truth or falsity of that well-known ballad, it would be hard to pronounce positively. The arguments *against* it are, that there is no mention made of it in any contemporary history; while, on the contrary, there is a letter of the earl's extant after his wife's death, speaking of her with much respect and affection. The arguments *for* it are the ballad itself, the air of which, known as "Lady Cassillis's Lilt," is very old, and is remarkable as the only one traceable to the wide county of Ayr. Besides, floating traditions like these are usually founded on *some* fact, if we could only rightly disentangle it. As to whether it was earl John's wife who committed the indiscretion, the ballad does not say, and I do not care to affirm. I only mean to hold by my opinion, that some time in the history of these old

Kennedys, an escapade like that narrated in the ballad took place, and which enables us to get away for a little out of the turmoil of brawls and fights into the romantic region of love.

The scene of the ballad, as is well known, was Cassillis House, on the banks of the Doon, about three miles from Maybole. This house originally consisted of a large square tower or peel, with walls of astonishing thickness. Before the door stood, and still stands, a magnificent Plane called the Dule tree, or tree of sorrow—so called, say some, because criminals were hanged upon it; or, as say others, because it was the tree beneath which the retainers used to assemble to make lamentation over the death of their Chief.* Below the ground floor there is a dungeon, whose sole entrance is by a trap-door opening from above. Some years ago, this place was cleared out, when several cart loads of human bones were removed, "the lingering witnesses, it is to be feared, of deeds and times long gone by, when the devoted guest or the refractory vassal went so frequently amissing, having met a fate which some might suspect, but none durst enquire into."

One day when Lord Cassillis was from home, the lady was surprised to hear a band of men singing at the castle gate. She came down to see them, and the result is thus given—

The gypsies cam' to oor gude lord's yett,
  And O, but they sang sweetly;
They sang sae sweet and sae very complete,
  That doon cam' oor fair lady.

And she cam' trippin' doon the stair,
  Wi' a' her maids before her;
As soon as they saw her weel-faured face,
  They cuist the glamour ower her.

* When David, first Earl of Cassillis, fell at the battle of Flodden in 1513, his fate was deplored for many days by his friends and retainers under the Dule tree of Cassillis.

"O, come wi' me," says Johnnie Faa,
"O, come wi' me, my dearie,
For I vow and I swear by the hilt o' my sword,
That your lord shall nae mair come near ye."

o o o o

And when oor lord cam' hame at e'en,
And speered for his fair lady,
The tane she cried, and the other replied,
"She 's awa' wi' the gypsy laddie."

"Gae saddle to me the black, black steed,
Gae saddle and mak' him ready,
Before that I either eat or sleep,
I 'll gae seek my fair lady."

And we were fifteen well-made men,
Although we werena bonny,
And we were a' put doon but ane,
For a fair, young, wanton lady.

I may merely add, that according to tradition, the lady, when brought back, was first compelled to witness the hanging of the gypsy party on the Dule tree, and was then imprisoned for life in the Castle of Maybole.

John, the seventh Earl of Cassillis, was a staunch Presbyterian, and suffered severely in purse during the persecution of the Covenant times.

It was Archibald, twelfth Earl of Cassillis, who was created first Marquess of Ailsa, in 1832.

The *Arms* of the Kennedy family are thus given—Argent, a chevron, gules, between three cross crosslets, fitchee, sable; all within a double tressure, flowered and counter-flowered in the second. *Crest*, a dolphin. *Supporters*, two swans, proper. *Motto, Avise la fin* (Consider the end).*

* The motto of the Shaw Kennedy family (Kirkmichael House) is interesting—*Malim esse probus quam haberi* (I had rather be honest than be counted honest).

The Castle, Maybole
(previous to recent alterations).

OUR ANCIENT HOUSES.

Far back, for noo six hundred years,
From ancient history appears,
This toon has stood amang its peers—
This auld toon o' Maybole.

When Girvan was a sandy knowe,
And Crosshill lay beneath the plough,
And Dailly stood—no one knows how,
Stood the auld toon o' Maybole.

There are many old buildings in our midst, any one of which would make the fortune of an ordinary town. Of course, these are gradually being removed to make way for more commodious ones; but there are still a goodly number left, and I cannot help expressing a wish that in some way the antique features of our town should not be utterly sacrificed in the rage for improvement. The old, though not convenient, is certainly picturesque; and it is a pity that beauty should be banished by comfort. Surely a way could be found for securing both, if people would go about it in the right fashion. I trust, therefore, that our Dean of Guild will see in future that the quaint features of our High Street, which are so rapidly disappearing, shall not be altogether forgotten or ignored in the new buildings that appear there.

The oldest house existing in Maybole is the *Collegiate Church*, which has stood now for upwards of five hundred years. This fact, of course, marks it out of itself; but besides that, the old ruin is famous as being the burying-place of nearly the whole line of the old "kings of Carrick," once so noisy and turbulent, now so quiet and peaceful.

Their bones are dust,
Their swords are rust,
Their souls are with the saints, we trust.

It is not likely that any more of the Ailsa family will be interred here, as the late Marquess expressed a wish to be buried within his own grounds, where, accordingly, he now lies. There is little to be seen inside the building except a plain marble tablet with the names of some of the family, beginning with John, the seventh earl, who died in 1701. Certain others of the local landed gentry, who assisted at one time in keeping the old church in repair, have the right of sepulture here; and the small square aisle, with the finely sculptured coats of arms, is the special burying-place of the lairds of Culzean, a family now merged in the Ailsa branch, and whose town house stood in High Street, at the corner of the Back Vennal, and was only removed about a dozen years ago. The *Holy Water Font* is still to be seen near the door, and the *Piscina* at the east end where the High Altar stood, while a sculptured tomb without a name adorns the wall opposite.

It was on the 19th of May, 1563, that Mass was last celebrated within the walls of the "Auld College." The act was illegal at the time in Scotland, and might have been punished severely. Nevertheless, a band of 200 Kennedys assembled here with arms in their hands on that day, and worshipped God in the old fashion. And one cannot help respecting them for it. It was the same principle that fired the hearts of the Covenanters afterwards, though shown in different guise. And there is a touch of pathos, too, about that gathering. It was the last public testimony to the old mode of faith. It was Carrick's Good-Night to the old scheme of things, before its face was finally turned to the wall.

But although the Collegiate Church is our oldest building, the one we are proudest of is the *Castle*, which so finely commands the town's entrance from the north. It is understood to have been built in 1560, as the town residence of the Lords of Cassillis. Robert Chambers says of it—"A finer, more sufficient, and more entire house of its kind, has never fallen under the notice of the present writer." The ground floor is vaulted in the ancient fashion, and such of the apartments as remain unaltered (as, for instance, the Countess's Room) still retain traces of their ancient grandeur. The Countess's Room is the one in the upper story with the oriel window looking up High Street. And as tradition is always ingenious in adapting itself to existing localities, the story has arisen that the sculptured heads, which so prettily adorn that window, are sculptured effigies of the gypsies who carried her off. In former times the door of the castle looked up High Street. The building has been consider-

to time, the last one being a new roof; which, however, has hardly been done in a style in keeping with the rest, and respecting which I lodged at the time the following protest:—

Our steeple is old, our steeple is grey,
It has served us well for many a day,
For more than two centuries it has stood
And faced the rain, and storm, and flood.
It has watched the growth of this town of ours,
And measured the march of the passing hours,
And laughed with our smiles, and wept with our tears,
This Steeple of more than two hundred years.

It has relics to show of the bygone Past:
The "Jouggs" which bound the culprit fast,
And the "Stocks" which bound him faster still,
When nought could tame his stubborn will;
And the old tinkling Bell which the Frenchman made,
Whose voice has gladdened both man and maid;
And the quaint old door looking down the street
To the "Lazy Corner" where idlers meet.

One winter night the wind blew high,
And bore disaster far and nigh;
The townsfolk rose with morning light
To see the damage of the night;
When lo! the Steeple-top was seen
A comic spectacle, I ween;
It looked athwart the morning sky
Like tippler's hat put on awry.

The top was doom'd: it must come down;
It was a danger to the town;
The very Cock that turn'd about
To show the way the wind was out,
Had now to bow to Fate's decree
And yield its post of dignity;
And so, with ropes securely bound,
'Twas brought all safely to the ground.

But now our Steeple look'd so bare
Expos'd thus to the wintry air,
That every townsman, Scot and Pat,
Wish'd well our Steeple a new Hat.
But what *sort* of a Hat should now be got
Was next the subject of deep thought—
"A Dome" cries one—"a Hat like those
Worn now-a-days by all the beaux."

"No hat at all," cries some mad wag,
"But Flagstaff tall to sport a flag;"
Whilst the most, to compliment the town,
Would only have an "Iron Crown."
So the Crown was bought and perched upon it,
Just like a small Glengarry bonnet,
And the weather-beaten Steeple grey
Was flouted by the crown so gay.

But had they asked the Steeple bare
What sort of a hat *it* wished to wear,
Its answer, I ween, could only be—
"Just give me the hat I used to see—
The old cocked-hat, with its cozy air,
And the Weather-cock above it there;
For an old-fashioned hat suits old-fashioned people,
And that 's just the case with your old Town Steeple."

What is known among us as *John Knox's House* is perhaps the only other ancient building of note remaining. It is the house in which the famous Debate between John Knox and the last Abbot of Crossraguel took place in 1562. It was formerly known as the Red Lion Inn, but has now more appropriately resumed its position as a private dwelling. At the time the debate took place in it, it was the residence of the Rev. Andrew Gray, at that time Provost of the Collegiate Church. Some have denied that the present house was the house in which the debate was held, but merely one built on its site. And they point to the modern appearance of the present house, as well as to the fact that a few years ago there was dug out of the ruins of the adjoining property a lintel stone with the following inscription :—

THREE D'S, THREE L'S WANTING AE I,
HARD YIER FOR KINGS, DUKS, LORDS, AND ME.

This couplet gives the date of the erection of the house in which it was found as 1649, but cannot very well invalidate the antiquity of Knox's house itself. The house has certainly been much modernised in appearance, but there are still traces of great antiquity about it. And the small windows, whose former position is still seen in the walls, the wide entrance hall with its quaint stone staircase now covered with wood, the old wooden panel still preserved in Knox's Room, and the pious lintel inscription on one of the houses behind; all point, I think, to an antiquity quite equal to that supposed.

The foregoing, however, are only a few of the mansions of the gentry that used to adorn our town. In former times there were twenty-eight stately dwellings in our midst, inhabited by the Carrick lairds, who used to make Maybole their place of residence, although it must be confessed that their dwellings rarely exceeded the accommodation of a modern villa, and sometimes not even that!

OUR STREETS AND THEIR NAMES.

Oor hooses may no be sae stately as mony,
Oor streets and oor lanes may be narrow in boun,
But the fact that we bide in 't mark'st oot frae a' ithers,
And gars us think much o' oor ain bit toon.

The principal street of our town is *High Street*, sometimes called Main Street—but I prefer the antique designation. Every town long ago had its High Street, from Edinburgh downwards; and our town used to begin and end with High Street and its dependencies. Whitehall, Welltrees Street, Newyards, and the Kirklands, were all suburbs then, and there is mention in the Council Records of certain persons who bought and sold goods in the street called the Kirklands, which lay *outside* the boundaries of the town, and which buying and selling sorely troubled the magistrates. It must be remembered that High Street, with the vennals running from it, form the antique portion of Maybole. This ancient street of ours has been considerably modified. Formerly the roadway was higher in the middle, while the ascent was steeper; and the Market Cross, standing in the centre on its elevated steps, must have given an air of dignity to it which now is wanting. The street seems to have remained uncausewayed until 1745, there being a Council Minute on 4th June that year, directing the inhabitants to "turn out and collect stones and sand; those who have horses to lead the same, and those who refuse to comply to be fined in eighteen shillings Scots for each absent day." *

The narrow street now called the Post Vennal was formerly called the *Foul* or dirty Vennal, and doubtless for sufficient reason. There is mention made in the Council Records of the Foul Vennal being causewayed in 1775, probably with a view to remedy its foulness.

The names *Kirk Wynd* and *Kirk Port* point to the fact that the Parish Church formerly stood in the old Churchyard. The Kirk Port used to be a genteel locality, and several of the country lairds had their town residences in it. In the second volume of Chambers's Journal there is a notice of one Will Dick, a Maybole thatcher, who had a gift of the gab which distinguished him. In describing a country "Kirn" at which he was present, he said :—"There was a chiel there, and he couldna be content wi' a dish, but he wad hae a turheen to himsel. And, man, ye never saw sic a supper o' curds in your born days. Od, they jist gaed owre his throat like dowgs driving sheep, or cluds gaun owre the mune, or the *Kirk Port when it's skailin'.*"

I do not know how the *Whitehall* came by its Royal name, but the *Kirklands* speaks for itself. And the *Newyards* tells us that it was formerly occupied by the gardens of some of the wealthier inhabitants of the town. The *School Vennal* formerly led up to the Parish School, and the *Ladyland Road* points to the fact that the ground thereabout at one time belonged to the Collegiate Church, which, as we know, was dedicated to our Blessed Lady, the Virgin Mary.

* Towards the foot of High Street there is an old four-storey house which had its origin in the following comical cause. The neighbouring proprietor was erecting a three-storey building which somewhat crowed over our friend. But he bided his time till the other was finished, and then quietly stripped off his roof and put on a *fourth* storey—not to boast over his neighbour—Oh no! but merely for the pious reason, "*that he had a gude Neebor abune!*" So was it in days of old.

The *Corral Glen* is properly the *Quarry* Glen, which it visibly is. The new road through it was opened about fifty years ago. Previously, the only entrance to the town from the Girvan valley led up through Welltrees Street. The old Scotch way of writing the word Quarry was Quarrle, from which we have the strange corruption of *Corral*, that so frequently puzzles strangers.

Welltrees Street explains itself; and the somewhat comical name of the *Kilndoup*, which it sometimes receives, arises from the circumstance that a malt-kiln used to stand at the head of it. Leading off from it is a lane called the *Croft*, but which is written in the Council Records *Croft-in-gea*, an old Gaelic name meaning the *Croft-of-the-Geese*, from the fact, probably, that these birds used to be pastured there in days of old.

Pat's Corner was so called after one Pat O'Hara, who lived there; and it would doubtless have shocked the reverend Abbots of Crossraguel very much, had they known that their town residence would have come to bear that designation. For Pat's corner is properly called *Abbot's Place;* and the kailyards behind were once so beautifully adorned that they received the flattering name of the *Garden of Eden.*

The *Public Green* of Maybole was formerly called the *Ball Green*, from the custom of playing ball on it. The privilege of grazing cows on it was annually let by the magistrates for a small sum—generally fifteen shillings. In 1819 the Earl of Cassillis of that day attempted to claim a right at law to the possession of this Green, but he was defeated.

And now, let us hear a description of our town as it appeared two hundred years ago to the enquiring eye of the Rev. William Abercrummie, then Episcopal parish minister here: "This towne of Mayboll stands upon an ascending ground, from east to west, and lyes open to the south. It hath one principall street (High St.) with houses upon both sydes, built of freestone; and it is beautifyed with the situation of two castles, one at each end of this street. That on the east belongs to the Erle of Cassilis; beyond which, eastward, stands a great new building, which be his granaries. On the west end is a castle, which belonged some time to the Laird of Blairquhan, which is now the Tolbuith, and is adorned with a pyremid, and a row of ballesters round it, raised from the top of the staircase, into which they have mounted a fyne clock. There be four lanes which passe from the principall street; one is called the Back Vennal, which is steep, declining to the south-east, and leads to a lower street (Weaver Vennal and Abbot Street), which is far larger than the high chiefe street, and it runs from the Kirkland to the Welltrees; in which there have been many pretty buildings belonging to the severall gentry of the countrey, who were wont to resort thither in winter, and divert themselves in converse together at their owne houses. It was once the principall street of the toune [Hold up your head, Abbot Street and the Vennal!]; but many of these houses of the gentry having been decayed and ruined, it has lost much of its ancient beauty. Just opposite to this Vennal (Back Vennal) there is another (School Vennal) that leads north-west from the chiefe street to the Green, which is a pleasant plott of ground, enclosed round with an earthen wall, wherein they were wont to play at football, but now at the gowffe and byasse-bowls. At the east end of the principall street are other two lanes; the one called Foull Vennal, carryes northward; the other farder east upon the chiefe street, passes to the south-east, and is called the Kirk Vennal, and is the great resort of the people from the toune to the church. The houses of this toune, on both sydes the street, have their several gardens belonging to them; and in the lower street there be some pretty orchards, that yield store of good fruit."

There is a place in ilka toon,
Weel kenn'd by a' the country roun',
Whaur gathers every idle loon,
And its ca'd the Lazy Corner.

The Tippler comin' aff the spree,
The tradesman glad his wark to flee,
And the man wha has naething else to dae,
Gang to the Lazy Corner.

It 's wonnerfu' the things they hear
Of a' that 's happen'd, far and near—
Whether they 're *true* 's a sma' affair
T' the folks at the Lazy Corner.

The corner wi' *ill* news is rife—
Wha's sent to jail—wha's threshed his wife—
Wha 's focht and nearly took a life—
Is food for the Lazy Corner.

The clishmaclaivers o' the toon,
The gossip o' the country roun',
Tittle-tattle—that 's the soun'
Has charms for the Lazy Corner.

Then, ilka body that gangs by
Maun stan' remarks—be 't lass or boy—
While winks, and nods, and glances sly
Mak' fun for the Lazy Corner.

Of course it 's richt that folk should talk—
But better, surely, tak' a walk,
Or by the fireside ca the crack,
Than stan' at the Lazy Corner.

For in this busy life o' man,
Whase length can hardly reach a span,
It 's surely wrang to idly stan'
At ony Lazy Corner.

THE WELLS OF MAYBOLE.

The old oaken bucket, the iron-bound bucket,
The moss-covered bucket, which hung in the well.

In former times, and before the necessity of obtaining water by gravitation for small towns was thought of, the wells of a town were of great importance, and were placed under the care of the magistrates. In our Council Records, there is faithful mention made every year of certain committees appointed as "visitors and inspectors of St. Cuthbert's well, and the water-race therefrom, as also of the spout of Welltrees, and the Lady Well." And I am informed that these committees are appointed annually still. In those times, carrying water was one of the chief duties of the household, and a pair of stoups behind the door was a necessary part of every workman's outfit.

The chief of our town wells was *St. Cuthbert's well*, so called from our patron saint; or *My Lord's well*, from being near the Castle. This was originally a draw-well with a stream of water running from it. But in 1804 a pump was put over it for greater convenience. As the expense of doing this was greater than the town-funds at that time would allow, the magistrates opened a public subscription, honestly alleging that "the funds of the town were small, and the demands thereon numerous." Some few years ago, in forming St. Cuthbert's Road, the old pump was removed and the present conspicuous one erected instead.

Next in importance after St. Cuthbert's well was the *Welltrees Spout*, our notable West-End well. To shew its importance to the town folk, there is mention made in the Council Records (1807) of the sum of £4 · 1 · 8 being paid to one John M'Clure for a piece of ground, in order to give the people better access to the place "where the water issues from the rock at the Spout of Welltrees." There was also, it appears, a small plot of ground, belonging to the town, let as a garden at the yearly rent of five shillings, which stood close by the well, and which I suppose is the place now so unornamentally enclosed with railway sleepers. The name of the Spout is plainly derived from the fine Ash tree which so picturesquely surmounts the spring. Some years ago it was calculated to give 10, 000 gallons of water per hour.

The *Lady Well* has risen into fame from our chief shoe factory being named from it. It rises at the foot of the Ladywell Brae, not far from the Welltrees Spout. It gets its name, like Ladyland, from our Lady the Virgin Mary, to whom it was dedicated, from being on the Collegiate Church grounds.

There was formerly a well in the Public Green, called the *Green Well*. Its position is marked by a flat stone near the late Mr Dykes's memorial fountain.

Tippersweill is the name given to an ancient Spring mentioned in local history. The road that now leads past it at one time formed part of the highway to Kirkoswald;

and not far off once stood *Peden's Thorn*, famous in covenanting traditions. *Tipper* or *Tobar*, means a well in Gaelic, but what *Sweill* means, remains a mystery.

There were two Holy wells in the neighbourhood of our town, both famous for the cure of diseases. One was *St. Helen's Well*, at Balloch mount, and believed to possess the power of curing sickly children if brought on May day. And the other was the well at *Pennyglen Cross*, which was believed to have the power of curing the muir-ill in cattle. But these Bethesdas are now out of date.

Finally, there is a well-known little Spout in the Quarry Glen, which all residenters in Maybole have a liking for, and in praise of which the following verses were written :—

In this drouthy warld there 's nocht to compare
  Wi' the water that comes frae the sky,
For washing your face, or makin your tea,
  Or slockening your drouth when you 're dry.
But of a' the waters that cheerily flow
  To bless bairns, women, and men,
There 's nane in this toon that 's at a' to compare
  Wi' the wee trinklin Spoot in the Glen.

The Welltrees is sweet, and it never rins dry,
  But it disna dae to be keepit owre lang;
And the auld Castle Well 's refreshing to drink,
  But it gangs gey an' aft oot o' fang.
And the Pipe-water—weel, the less that is said
  Aboot *that* the better, we ken;
But for a gude drink to cule your dry mou,
  Commend *me* to the Spoot in the Glen.

It 's no vera big—it 's jist a *wee* spoot
  That comes oot o' the breist o' the brae,
But it 's sweet, and it 's cule, and it 's pure as the snaw
  That comes frae the clouds far away.

And it's free to a' comers—the bairns wi' their cans,
  And a' folks aboot the West en';
Even the rouch carter lads will pu' up their carts
  And tak a gude swig at the Glen.

There's a great deal o' drink that's no vera gude,
  And brings meikle sorrow and shame,
It steals awa health, and your money to buit,
  And lea's ye a sair ruined name.
But the Drink that I praise has nae siccan fauts;
  It'll no land ye in the prison's dark den,
And ye'll no hae your heid sair, or your jacket in rags,
  If ye stick by the Spoot at the Glen.

There's mony a ane in a far distant land
  Wha minds hoo, in youth's sunny day,
They gaed wi' their stoups, and ca'd their bit crack,
  At the place whaur the wee Spoot's to-day.
And there's mony a ane's gane farther awa',
  Wha asked on his deathbed to sen'
For a jug o' the cule, cule water that rins
  Frae the wee trinklin Spoot in the Glen.

And the wee Spoot aye rins, year in and year oot,
  And it asks neither fame nor a fee,
Content if it slockens the drouth o' the weans,
  And maks your drap parritch or tea.
And the lesson it teaches to young and to auld,
  Frae childhood to threescore and ten,
Is, "Do what ye can, and ne'er think o' reward,"
  Jist like the wee Spoot in the Glen.

Modern Maybole is not dependent on its wells as of yore. It now has a water supply brought from Loch Spouts, a distance of 3½ miles. This of course is a great boon to the town, but it was bought very dearly; the slump sum of £11,000, having been paid for the new and old water-works. But we must march with the times. The old-fashioned *gang of water* could not now content us. And so we must e'en turn on the tap both on water-pipe and purse!

OUR CEMETERIES.

O come, come wi' me to the auld kirkyard,'
We well know the path thro' the soft greensward;
Friends slumber there we were wont to regard,
We will trace out their names in the auld kirkyard.

The Old Churchyard stands in the centre of the town, and is now closed for interments save in the case of special exceptions. The church itself stood in the centre of the churchyard, a little to the left of the present entrance, and its site may still be traced. Two hundred years ago, it was built in the shape of the letter T, with the parish school at the east end of it, separated by a partition of wood. This old church was superseded by a large mean looking structure, which, however, only stood for some 54 years, when it was replaced by the present erection, built in 1809, outside the churchyard altogether.

This churchyard has now been used as a place of burial for nearly 700 years. Roman Catholics and Protestants all lie there undistinguished. There are at present about 200 tombstones in it; but that number is insignificant compared with the number who must actually be sleeping there. Reckoning the average number of burials per year, for the last 700 years, at only one-fourth of what they now are, there will be about 20,000 persons sleeping in that little half acre of ground. Most of the tombstones are facing the East, in accordance with the old belief that Christ will appear in the East on the resurrection morning. The oldest stone is near the west wall, and bears this inscription:—"Heir lyis ane honest man, Moreis Makmorrie, and his spous, quha deceist in ye last of October, 1618"—*i.e.*, 267 years ago. The stone is in excellent preservation, having been recently renovated.

Nearly opposite the entrance, on the off-side, is a large *through-stane*, bearing the following lines:—

Under the neighbouring monument lies
The golden dust of man and wife,
Of pious line, both soon shall rise,
To long-expected, glorious life.
They for their constancy and zeal,
Still to the back, did proved good steel
For our Lord's royal truths and laws
The ancient covenanted cause
Of Scotland's famous Reformation,
Declining laws of usurpation.

The man's name was John M'Lymont, who lived in Auchalton, and died the 1st of Nov., 1714, aged 69. Mr

M'Clymont, at present tenant in Balsaggart, is descended from this worthy, and has given me the following particulars regarding him. John M'Lymont of Auchalton was a noted covenanter, and was sorely persecuted. On one occasion his house was burned over his head, and he and his family had to hide on Glenalla moor, where a watch was set on them for several days, so that they were exposed to great extremities of cold and hunger. For four years he could not sleep in safety in his own house; but at last the clouds rolled away, and the old man and his wife were allowed to die quietly, and be buried in peace and honour. The name, however, had been forgotten, until the present Mr M'Clymont's father caused a search to be made for the tombstone, and it was found unharmed, but completely sunk in the earth. It has now been restored. An old sword was found in the thatch of Auchalton, which is supposed to have belonged to the covenanting hero.

Near the gateway of the churchyard is a stone to the memory of David Dunn, schoolmaster in Maybole. This Mr Dunn was a leading magistrate of the town in his day, and is mentioned as one of those "worthy fellows" whom Burns met on his visit to Maybole in 1786. There are also several tombstones of ministers, with the usual fulsome inscription, which is our Scotch way of canonization. On the site of the old church there is a neat granite stone with the inscription:—"In memory of William Niven of Kirkbride, deceased 18th Nov., 1844, aged 85; and of his wife Isabella C. Niven, deceased 15th Feb., 1841, aged 68. Their mortal remains are laid here." William Niven was a school-fellow of Burns's at Kirkoswald; he afterwards became the leading personage in the town, and many quaint stories are told of his self-importance. At least *one* of the tombstones here has no inscription at all on it; and several others have merely the name of the persons who erected them, without any mention of those who are buried there—an affecting reminder to us how soon we are forgotten once we are beneath the sod; for, while we may erect a tombstone to mark our grave, we can't very well insert the inscription on it.

The *New Cemetery* was opened in 1851, and was enlarged a few years ago. The first interment was that of the wife of the Rev. Mr Dodds, Free Church minister. Dr Menzies and the Rev. Mr Moir now lie here, as also Mr Dykes of the Castle, Dr M'Tyer, Bailie Sinclair, Provost Gray, and many others whose names are well remembered among us. Within the grounds of the Free Church, one of the former physicians of the town lies buried; but this example has not been followed. A few interments annually take place in the old churchyard of Kirkbride, near Dunure, and a few within the walls of the Old Collegiate Church, but the great mass are now laid in the New Cemetery; so that we may say of it with Longfellow—

> Into its furrows shall we all be cast,
> In the sure faith that we shall rise again
> At the Great Harvest, when the archangel's blast
> Shall winnow, like a fan, the chaff and grain.

A Covenanters' Conventicle.

OUR MINISTERS.

At church, with meek and unaffected grace,
His looks adorned the venerable place;
Truth from his lips prevailed with double sway,
And fools, who came to scoff, remained to pray.

Maybole has always been conspicuously Protestant. Ever since John Knox shook the rafters of the Back Vennal in his debate with Abbot Kennedy, the men of our town have cherished the doctrines of the Reformation. And not only have they done so in favourable times, but in unfavourable times. Maybole was a known centre of the Covenanting Cause. Most of the gentry, and nearly all the common people, were favourable to the Covenant; and in the Antiquarian Museum, Edinburgh, there is exhibited the original National Covenant signed by the parishioners of Maybole, declaring their adherence to the national faith. When the dark days set in, Maybole was not found wanting in courage.* The field adjoining Gardenrose Toll was known by the name of the *Muster Lea*, because the Covenanters of Carrick mustered there in 1679, before marching off to Bothwell Bridge. Richard Cameron preached here to many thousands, and dispensed the sacrament of the Lord's Supper in the open fields, for the first time, among the Covenanters. And there once stood in a wood near Ladycross Toll, until thoughtless indifference destroyed it, a large boulder stone called *Cargill's Stone*, which served as the Communion Table to a great gathering of the Covenanters in 1681. This meeting was illegal at the time; and attendance at it formed one of the articles of the indictment against several of our martyrs. It was also one of the last of the Coventicles addressed by Donald Cargill, he having been seized and hanged at Edinburgh a few months afterwards. A few fragments of Cargill's stone may still be seen at a field gate on the farm of that name.

The first minister of Maybole after the Reformation seems

* "Last week there was a fair at Maybole, where a great many swords were sold."—*Report to Government, Nov., 1677.*

"We have now every other day frequent Conventicles, but on Sunday last there was a Conventicle in Carrick that the like hath not been seen in Scotland; for there were, as is said, about 600 well-appointed men in arms, and above 7000 common people, so that in all probability they will rise in rebellion."—*Extract from private letter, dated 6th August, 1678.*

to have been the Rev. John M'Corne, who was translated from Dalmellington in 1595. But the first noted one was the Rev. James Bonar, (ancestor of the present celebrated Bonars of the Free Church), who came among us in 1608. Mr Bonar was a person of learning, a leader among the Covenanting party, and was elected Moderator of the General Assembly in 1644. He was rich and generous, and mention is made of his having added an aisle to the Parish church at his own expense, as well as giving 150 marks towards the Glasgow College Library. A strange story is recorded of his having been appointed to go to Stoneykirk in Galloway, to induct a minister there; but when he went, "there arose such an opposition from the women and others, armed with clubs and stones, that he was prevented from preaching within the Kirk, and the tumult so wrought on his mind that it cast him into a long and dangerous fever." The following General Assembly appointed a Committee to meet at Ayr for the trial of the rioters.

At the time of the Covenanting persecution, the minister of Maybole was the Rev. Mr Hutchison, inducted in 1655. For his Covenanting principles he was deprived of his benefice in 1616, rigorously dealt with in 1669, indulged at Dundee 1672, and finally restored to his old church of Maybole in 1690. During the Episcopal intrusion, two curates seem to have lived here. One was Mr John Jaffray, who was expelled for bad conduct in 1670. The other was Mr William Abercrummie, who wrote a very interesting account of Carrick, which has been preserved. All historians of Carrick must be grateful to Mr Abercrummie for his little treatise.

Our most noted minister, however, was the Rev. James MacKnight, son of the minister of Irvine, inducted in 1753. This man was a superior scholar, a liberal, wise, and prudent ecclesiastic, and one of the most respectable writers the

Church of Scotland has produced. His principal works were:—"Harmony of the Four Gospels." "The truth of the Gospel History," and "A new translation of the Apostolical Epistles, with Commentary and notes." He became Moderator of the General Assembly in 1769, was translated to Jedburgh same year, afterwards to Edinburgh in 1772, and died in 1800. It was concerning his "Harmony" that the Maybole blacksmith passed the criticism, "Oor minister has been trying to mak four men agree wha never cast oot." And it was of his preaching the witty remark was made in allusion to his wet clothes, "Never mind, Doctor, ye'se be dry aneuch when ye get into the pu'pit."

Of the Rev. James Wright, inducted here in 1770, the following curious anecdote is recorded. "Having stated from the pulpit at the close of Divine Service on a Sabbath forenoon in harvest, 1807, that he conceived a favourable opportunity to save the crops, then in much danger, was vouchsafed by Providence, from a temporary change in the weather; and that, therefore, those who chose to devote the afternoon to that work of necessity might, in his opinion, do so without violation of the Sabbath, a *fama* arose, which was brought under the notice of the Presbytery, and an enquiry appointed. On an appeal taken to the Synod, they agreed, in October, 1808, to set aside the whole proceedings of the Presbytery in the business—at the same time, sensible of the importance of the sanctification of the Sabbath, they recommend to all the members within their bounds, to be particularly attentive to it, and to beware how far they allow of cases of necessity, which may form a stumbling-block to any of their parishioners." Dr. Wright, in this matter, seems to have been supported by the town; as there was a petition forwarded to the Synod, signed by the Magistrates, stating that, in their opinion, there was no ground for any enquiry. They stated that on the

Sabbath in question, the minister, after intimating as above, requested a show of hands as to how many desired to work, and seeing there were few, he gave notice that there would be afternoon service as usual. They also inform the Synod that "for the last two years the people of the parish would have been deprived of public worship upon the Lord's-day, in consequence of their being no church in which they could be assembled (the old one being ruinous), had not the minister, though aged and infirm, proposed to meet his people in the open air, which he has done without the intermission of a single day, however inclement the weather, to as large a congregation almost as formerly."

Within the present century, our parish ministers have been Charles Logan, 1813 to 1823; John Paul from Straiton in 1823, and translated to St. Cuthbert's, Edinburgh, in 1828; and George Gray, from Eckford, in 1828, and appointed Professor of Hebrew in Glasgow University, 1840. The rest are in the memory of all.

Johnnie Stuffie.

OUR TOWN CHARACTERS.

Great wits are sure to madness near allied,
And thin partitions do their bounds divide.

Our town was long famous for its "characters," and it may be worth while, in these monotonous days, to jot down a few sayings of those among us in former times, who were accounted *originals* after their fashion.

Will Gordon was town officer in his day. Being at a roup at Kilhenzie, he was offered some drink, which he had not declined. Sir Adam Fergusson of Kilkerran, passing by, accosted him:—"Ah Gordon! you should never drink so early in the day." "'Deed, Sir Adam," said Gordon, "*you can drink when you like, but I maun drink when I can get it.*" One wintry day Gordon found himself very drouthy at Slateford, and going into the public house there, he "drank his shoes." When stepping out again, he was heard thus to soliloquise, "Step forrit, barefit Gordon, if it's no *ón* ye, it's *in* ye!"

Dr M'Cann was an Irish itinerant herbalist, who died in the Poor's House about twenty years ago. He confined himself chiefly to children's diseases, and his boast was that he could cure everything except "*the raal die.*" His usual remark after a diagnosis was—"*Give me sixpence and a bottle and I'll cure the child.*" Some one, inquiring one day where he was going to, was answered—"I am going to Kirkoswald, *but have to stop two could favers on the road.*" To a patient he once remarked candidly—"I could not cure you; no man could do that—but I think, *I could cobble you up to the month of March.*" He was of course a little jealous of licensed practitioners, and was wont to remark—"The man was getting on well under my care, but *he took to riglar doctors, and so he died.*"

Old Dr Girvan is kindly remembered in the town for his wit and skill. On one occasion, however, he had swallowed some solution of arsenic by mistake, and his wife in great haste sent for the other two doctors of the town. Dr Macfarlane arrived first, but was so agitated that he did not know what to do. When Dr M'Tyer arrived, Dr Girvan coolly looked out from the bed, and said to him, "*Doctor, whether do you think it's Macfarlane or me has ta'en the pushon?*" On one occasion, the doctor came off second best. He somehow had great faith in mesmerism, and one day took up a wager of a gill of whisky with a brother physician that he could mesmerise him. A public house was soon entered, and the gill called for, and the operator at once proceeded to work. In a short time the disbeliever went off into a dose, to the intense delight of the old doctor, who quietly stepped out to call in witnesses. The sleeping man was soon aroused by the usual passes, and the gill-stoup was raised to pass round, when lo! it was discovered that the mesmerised man had seized the opportunity of the doctor's absence *to drink its contents!*

Several stories are given by Dean Ramsay, illustrating the grim wit of our countrymen as displayed at funerals; but none of them are better in their way than that mentioned to me by the late Rev. Mr Moir. He had been at a funeral in the Colmonell district; and, by way of starting a conversation, had remarked to a quiet farmer-looking man standing beside him, that the old drinking customs at funerals were passing away. But the answer he received was scarcely what he expected—"*Deed ay, man, a funeral's no worth gaun to nooadays.*" The tone of this reply reminds me of a remark attributed to a former Straiton innkeeper—"*I wad rather hae a Patna funeral than a Straiton waddin' ony day.*" And this again reminds me of a reply once given by a farmer, from whom I was asking a small favour, on the plea that I had officiated at three marriages in his house: "Three marriages! that's naething; *ye've been at three funerals!*"

Our forefathers, in a quiet country town like this, did business very cannily. The great credit system was then in its infancy, and was little believed in—a fact which one of our old worthies thus notified on his sign board:—

Since man to man is so unjust,
I scarcely know which one to trust;
I've often trusted to my sorrow—
Pay me to-day, and I'll trust you to-morrow.

But canny as our shopkeepers were, our farmers could match them. A farmer in Daltamie had a hill which he let for grazing purposes. A grazier went to take a look at it, but was disappointed with the bareness of the pasture. On stating this objection, the farmer replied quite cheerfully, "Oh, but ye see, *they'll hae plenty o' water, and a gran' view!*"

In these days "Naturals" are confined; but in former times they were not only tolerated but liked. Each town and village had one or more of its own whom every one knew, and every one spoke to. Rab Hamilton was the Ayr Natural, who used to sit on Sundays at the head of the pulpit stairs. One day he had put his head incautiously between the rails, and could not get it back again. Instantly the whole congregation was aroused by a loud voice crying out—"*Murder! my heid'll hae to be cuttit aff! Holy minister! Congregation! O, my heid maun be cuttit aff!*" When rescued, and asked what made him put his head there, he said, "It was jist to look on wi' *anither woman.*" Another natural, who sat on Ayr Bridge begging from the passers-by, used this convincing appeal: "I'm a puir man, and *can neither work nor want.*" And our own John Allan, who died a short while ago in the Poorhouse, asked a friend to write to some of his relatives for a little money. "But you *have* some siller, John?" "Weel, I hae fower shillings, but *that's unco little for a deein' man to hae!*"

But chief of our Maybole Naturals in times gone by was John M'Lymont, popularly and rather profanely known as Johnnie Stuffie. Johnnie was a little body, always dressed in a hat very much the worse of the wear, and a coat whose tails approached the ground much nearer than was ever designed by the tailor. The late Mr Porteous, printer, thus describes him:—"John M'Lymont, *alias* Johnnie Stuffie, a little, half-witted body, a native of Maybole, who, nevertheless (?) sometimes expressed wise sayings. He lived in a room by himself, and had a great fancy to accumulate a large wardrobe of very diverse patterns. He died in the year 1847, aged eighty-four years."

Johnnie's usual occupation was carrying water and going errands. He was a heavy snuffer. His invariable seat in the church was at the head of the pulpit stairs; and when once requested by the minister to take his seat somewhere else, he quietly replied that he would maybe come *nearer* instead. He was a singer in his way, and his favourite melody was, "O mother, dear, Jerusalem," which he used to sing to his friends for a consideration. Many are the stories told of poor Johnnie:—Being asked to go for a "gang" of water one Saturday night, he replied, "Man, I'm unco busy the nicht, but if ye could *pit ower till Monday,* I 'll mak' ye sure o 't then." Meeting a servant girl one day, the following conversation ensued: "Johnnie, div ye ken ye 're a fule?"—"Weel," said he, "there 's this differ atween us. *I'm a fule o' God's makin', and ye 're a fule o' your ain makin'.*" Somebody asked Johnnie, one day, how much money he had in the Bank? Johnnie replied seriously, "There 's naebody kens that but *God Almichty and Mr Niven.*" The late Rev. Mr Inglis was at one time elder in the Parish Church, and one day Johnnie accosted him, "Mr Inglis, ye never veesit me."—"No, Johnnie; but you 're not in my district."—"Sir, div ye think there 'll be ony deestricts in heevin?" Meeting the Rev. Dr. Paul, then minister of Maybole, Johnnie stopped him and said, "Sir, I wad like to speer a quastion at ye on a subject that's troublin' me."—"Well, Johnnie, what 's the question?"—"Sir, is 't lawfu' at ony time to tell a lee?"—"No, Johnnie, lies are never lawful."—"Weel," said Johnnie, "*Whether is't waur to tell a lee to keep doon a din, or to tell the truth to kick up a deevilment o' a din?*"—a question which may fairly be allowed capable of puzzling wiser heads than Johnnie's.

In going errands to farm houses, he was always sure of a bite and sup, but he was not easily satisfied. "Noo, Mrs G—, I wad like a bit o' your scone, for its unco gude, and a wee drap o' your sour, ye ken." But the scone and the milk never went down at the same time. There was always sure to be a supplement required. "I hae some sour left yet, Mrs G—, and I wad jist like a bit mair scone to it, ye ken." On one occasion, however, his greed brought him to grief. He was in the habit of attending the yearly communion services in the parishes around, and was always a guest at dinner in the manse kitchen. On one occasion he had been at Kirkmichael, and had contrived during mealtime to stuff his hat, which he kept under the table, full of meat and bread. But, ohone! he had filled the beadle's hat instead of his own, and so when the company broke up, the cat was out of the poke. Poor Johnnie was forbidden ever afterwards to dine at the minister of Kirkmichael's expense. A farmer's wife one day set before him a bowl of milk only, but Johnnie was equal to the occasion:—"*Mistress, that milk has an unco smell o' scone aboot it.*" When a plate of soup with meat and potatoes was set before him, he would say:—"*I'll jist mix them a' thegither, mistress, for they're a' gaun the ae road.*"

Johnnie lived for a considerable time in a house which stood where the Commercial Hall now stands. Afterwards, he removed to a small house at the Greenhead, and latterly to Inch's Close. When unable to take care of himself, he was removed to the house of a relative in Crosshill, where he died. He now lies in the old churchyard, in the burying place of one of our most respectable townsfolk, who kindly gave him a grave.

A queer wee man, wi' simple air,
Was Johnnie Stuffie,
Weel kenn'd alike by rich and puir
Was Johnnie Stuffie.
The water-carrier o' the toon,
The messenger to a' aroun',
And the butt o' every idle loon
Was Johnnie Stuffie.

Nae common bonnet croon'd the heid
O' Johnnie Stuffie,
But auld lum-hat was there instead
To Johnnie Stuffie;
A lang great-coat, ance thocht genteel,
Ay wrapped him roun' frae neck to heel,
Which only did the feet reveal
O' Johnnie Stuffie.

On Sabbath days, first at the kirk
Was Johnnie Stuffie,
Wi' weel brushed hat and weel washed sark
Cam' Johnnie Stuffie;
But no amang the rest sat he,
But on the pulpit steps sae hie,
The congregation a' could see
Bauld Johnnie Stuffie.

But a' folks dee, and 'mang the lave
Maun Johnnie Stuffie,
He rests noo in his quiet grave,
Wee Johnnie Stuffie;
Nae mair he'll stand the idle jeer,
Nor answer gie baith quaint and queer:
Though girr and water-stoups are here—
Whaur's Johnnie Stuffie?

Memorial Fountain, Public Green.

MODERN MAYBOLE.

Up wi' the sutors o' Selkirk,
And doon wi' the Earl o' Hume,
And up wi' ilka braw callant
That sews the single-soled shoon.

Maybole, in these days, has became famous for shoemaking. For many years it was a chief seat of the hand-loom weaving, but that industry has died a natural death among us, and in its stead has sprung up the leather trade, which has made the name of Maybole known all over the country.

Go where you will through Scotia's land,
You 'll see our shoes on every hand,
It 's Maybole on which Scotchmen stand,
The auld toon o' Maybole.

A short while ago it was calculated that 1200 persons were engaged in this industry in Maybole, who turn out upwards of 12,000 pairs of shoes every week, or the enormous amount of 600,000 pairs every year!

To dispose of this immense stock of shoe leather, a network of shops is spread over Scotland, and even over a part of England and Ireland, so that you can hardly go into the most remote corner of the country without seeing MAYBOLE SHOE SHOP staring you in the face.

One of the former ministers of Maybole used to relate how, in turning up a gazetteer to find out something concerning our town, he was shocked to read this sentence:—"Maybole is famous for weaving and thieving." Whatever it was in the past, I am glad to say that nowadays Maybole is wonderfully clear of thieving; and I suppose I may add that I am thankful it is as clear of weaving too. For that trade, once flourishing and well paid, had latterly been reduced to starvation point; so that it was with great gratitude the town hailed the introduction of the shoemaking industry, which was chiefly brought about by the exertions of Messrs Gray and Crawford. Maybole is also famous for the manufacture of Agricultural implements. The Messrs Jack and Mr Hunter hold a first place at all Shows and Competitions; and their works here are fitted up with most ingeniously contrived machinery.

Maybole is well supplied with churches. The Parish church, built in 1809, has 1200 sittings.* The Free Church, built in 1844, contains 950 sittings. The West Church, built in 1842, contains 640 sittings. The United Presbyterian Church, built in 1880, contains 400 sittings. Besides these there is a small Episcopal Church, an exceedingly neat Roman Catholic Church, a Methodist Chapel, an Evangelistic Hall, and a meeting place for "The Brethren."

The town stands on the slope of a hill, 300 feet above sea level. From almost any part of it, a fine view may be had of the country around; although, perhaps, the two finest view-points are Gallowhill and St. Murray Toll. Behind the town stands Mochrum Hill, 886 feet high, seen and known from afar. In front lies what Dr. Guthrie called "a fine, rolling country," stretching away to the hills of Straiton and Dalmellington. In the far horizon may be discerned Shalloch-on-Minnock (2520 feet) on the outskirts of Ayrshire, and Cairnsmore-of-Carsphairn (2597 feet) in Galloway—these being the highest hills in sight. On Kildoon hill stands a monument erected by the tenantry to the memory of Sir Charles Fergusson, Bart. of Kilkerran; while on Craigengower, above Straiton village, stands a similar tribute to the memory of Colonel Blair of Blairquhan, who fell at Inkermann. Overlooking the town from behind is the Gallowhill, where criminals used to be hanged in the days when the Earls of Cassillis held the Bailiery of Carrick. The last criminal put to death here was one Thomas Nilson, hanged in 1718, for "killing his

* Everybody knows that the steeple of this church is not particularly handsome. One day the late Bailie Sinclair was passing along the Newyards in company with the late Lord Ailsa, and called his lordship's attention to the fact that there was no clock on the steeple. "My lord, dae ye no think *that* steeple would be the better of a nock?" "Yes, said his lordship, I do think it would be the better of a good many *knocks*. It would be the better of a *knockdown*, I think."

neebor with ane dike-spade." In 1747, heritable jurisdictions were abolished throughout the country, Lord Cassillis receiving £1800 as compensation.

Maybole was long a lightly taxed community; but it is now rapidly making up lee-way, like the rest of the towns around. Not to speak of poor-rates and other local taxes, we have a public debt which has grown surprisingly on us of late. The various Board Schools have cost the parish £7,000; the water supply from first to last has cost £11,000; and the new drainage scheme will cost, when finished, at least £4,000; making in all the large sum of £22,000, for which this small community is responsible.

Maybole has few notable buildings except those of ancient date. Still the Public School, built in 1876, at a total cost of £6,000, is a handsome enough edifice of its kind. It has accommodation at present for about 850 scholars, and this is scarcely sufficient. The Royal Bank, built in 1858, at a cost of £3,700, is a set-off to the town. And on the Public Green, a very chaste Memorial Fountain of Peterhead Granite, 17 feet in height, has been recently erected with the following inscription: "In loving and affectionate remembrance of Thomas Dykes, Esquire, who for over forty years resided in Maybole, and died there, 12th June, 1879. Erected by his daughter."

The youth of Maybole were formerly taught in four schools, scattered over the town. These were the Parish School, West Church School,* Free Church School, and Industrial School, Greenhead. All these were finally closed in August, 1876, when the new Public School was opened. To those who were educated under the old *regime*,

* The West Church School, or "Carrick Academy," as it was sometimes called, had at one time a very defective floor. Occasionally a shriek would be heard from some part of the school, a startled pause, and then a boy would come running up, "Maister, there's anither lassie's leg through the flure!"

the following lines, written on the above occasion, may be suggestive:—

O the Auld Schule, the Auld Schule,
  What though the place was wee!
O happy hearts were gathered there
  When life was fu' o' glee.
Thy playground is deserted noo,
  Thy wa's are silent a',
But mony a happy memory
  Does that Auld Schule reca'.

O the Auld Schule, the Auld Schule!
  Thy forms were gettin' frail,
Thy desks were rough and shaky too,
  Thy floor was like to fail.
But richt gude wark was done in thee,
  And lessons taught wi' skill,
And clever men and women bright
  Were trained in that Auld Schule.

O the New Schule, the New Schule!
  Ye 're unco fine and crouse,
Ye 're a great credit to the toon,
  Oor ain new, grand Schulehoose.
But the Auld Schule, the Auld Schule!
  Forsaken though ye be,
There ne'er will be a New Schule
  Will seem the same to me.

The population of the parish of Maybole in 1871 was 5,895; while in 1881 it was 6,622, shewing an increase of 727. The district is usually healthy; the average deaths being only 130 annually, while there are 250 births and 45 marriages. With the return of prosperity, a better style of houses is being built and a greater measure of comfort secured. Local affairs are managed by a Provost and twelve

Police Commissioners—although the old Bailies and Town Council still continue. The Poorhouse has accommodation for 48 inmates, but these are spread over the parishes of Maybole, Kirkoswald, Kirkmichael, Girvan, Dailly, and Barr. There is also a Fever Hospital for cases of infectious diseases, but it is generally empty. There are two Fairs held annually, on the third Thursday of April and October.

PLACES OF INTEREST AROUND MAYBOLE.

'Mid pleasures and palaces, though we may roam,
Be it ever so humble, there's no place like home.
A charm from the skies seems to hallow us there,
Which, seek through the world, is ne'er met with elsewhere.

Lady Glen is perhaps the gem of the spots of interest about Maybole. It is within the grounds of Kilkerran House, and is, by permission of Sir James Fergusson, open to the public. The nearest station is Kilkerran, four miles from Maybole. The Glen itself forms a charming walk of about two miles or so. The ruins of an old chapel, dedicated to Our Lady, the Virgin Mary, still remain near the foot of the Glen, and several giant specimens of the silver fir *(picea pectinata)*, 12 feet in girth and upwards of 100 feet in height, cannot fail to be admired. With the exception of the Ness Glen, near Dalmellington, the Lady Glen is the prettiest in this district, and should be visited by every one.

Kirkmichael is a neat village of about 300 people, within three miles of Maybole. It is charmingly situated, and the old churchyard, with its encircling burn and embowering trees, is one of the prettiest to be seen anywhere. There is a martyr's tombstone in it, the lettering of which is said to have been the work of "Old Mortality." The oldest tombstone in Carrick is here, bearing the following inscription:

HIR LYIS QUINTINE MUIR OF GUD MEMORE
AND AGNIS BLAIR HIS SPOUIS. 1506.

The porch at the churchyard entrance is the only specimen in Carrick of a Lych or Corpse-gate.

Dalrymple is another pretty village, situated on the Doon, five miles from Maybole. On the road to it we pass Cassillis House, the scene of the ballad of Johnnie Faa, surrounded by its woods. A little way off is Skeldon Mills, on the Doon, producing weekly the comfortable number of 1,000 pairs of blankets. Dalrymple has a very neat Parish Church.

Straiton, seven miles from Maybole, is perhaps more prettily situated than either Kirkmichael or Dalrymple; although it is almost as difficult to decide between them as between the "three Graces," or the famous three whom Paris had to decide between in days of old. Straiton is finely encircled by hills. Its church possesses a very handsome aisle, which probably formed part of the old Roman Catholic church of the Parish. Lamaughty Glen is well worthy of a visit, and the view from the top of Craigengower will well repay the climb. The inscription on Colonel Blair's monument is as follows:—"Sacred to the memory of James Hunter Blair, younger of Blairquhan, Lieutenant-Colonel Scots Fusilier Guards, and Member of Parliament for this County, who fell in the gallant discharge of his duty on the field of

Inkermann, 5th Nov., 1854." About four miles farther up the river is Tairlaw Linn, where the Girvan takes a leap of sixty feet into a romantic gorge.

Between Straiton and Kirkmichael are the two stately castles of *Blairquhan* and *Cloncaird.* It is here where the Girvan looks its best. Elsewhere its course is smooth, but here it shews itself the true *Garbh abhain* or Rough river. Blairquhan is the handsomest residence in the Girvan Valley, and is designed after what is called the Tudor style.

Kirkoswald lies four miles west of Maybole. It was here Robert Burns attended the school of Hugh Rodger to study mathematics. His mother belonged to Craigenton in this parish, and the tombstone of the family, recently renovated under the care of Dr. Rogers of Edinburgh, may still be seen in the churchyard. "Tam o' Shanter's" tombstone (properly called Douglas Graham) and that of the old schoolmaster are both close by the tomb of the Browns, from whom Burns came.

Maidens is a pretty village on the sea-shore, about six miles from Maybole, and much frequented in the summer season for sea bathing. A shipbuilding yard has been recently erected here. About a mile from it is Turnberry Lighthouse, built on the site of Turnberry Castle, once the seat of the Earls of Carrick, and the probable birthplace of King Robert the Bruce. Close by is the site of Shanter farm. *Maidens* gets its name from the rocks off the shore, which are frequently so called in Scotland.

Culzean Castle, the seat of the Marquess of Ailsa, is about four miles from Maybole. It stands grandly on a rock overlooking the sea, and this rock is pierced by a number of caves, which penetrate a long way inland. A tradition goes to the effect, that a piper lost his way in one of them, and that his pipes were heard sounding beneath the ground as far as Straiton ! The old name of the house was *Cove.* The grounds are open to the public twice a week, on application to Mr Smith, Factor.

Dunure is a little village of fishermen, clustered around the old castle of Dunure, once the stronghold of the proud Kennedys. It was in this ruined fortress that Commendator Stewart of Crossraguel was roasted before a fire to compel him to assign his lands to Lord Cassillis. The little village looks snug enough, but seems cramped for want of room. The drive along the shore here, with the grand outlook on the Arran hills, Ailsa, and Cantire, is simply magnificent. Very beautiful, too, is the view of the bay of Ayr, from the top of Lagg brae. Dunduff, an unfinished tower belonging to the 17th century, is passed on the road; as also the old churchyard of *Kirkbride*.

Burns's Monument is within six miles of Maybole. It originated in a public meeting called by a few admirers of the poet; but which is said to have been attended by only two or three persons. Nothing daunted, various resolutions were moved and carried, subscription sheets issued, and the result is before us. The admission charge is twopence. The most precious of the relics to be seen within are the identical two half-Bibles presented, with a lock of his hair, by Burns to Highland Mary, on that memorable Sunday afternoon, so pathetically recorded in "Mary in Heaven." In a corner of the grounds are to be seen the statues of Tam o' Shanter and Souter Johnnie, executed by a mason in Ayr of the name of Thom.

On the road to Ayr, in passing the entrance to Blairston farm, there may be seen within an enclosing wall a *boulder stone* with a cross rudely carved on it, and commonly known as Wallace's stone. The cross is traditionally alleged to have been the work of a "venerable churchman, who did mediate a peace betwixt the Picts and Scots, and to give the more authority to his proposals, did in their sight, by laying a cross upon the stone, imprint that figure thereon." If any one doubts the truth of this story, let him go and see the stone for himself!

Middle Auchendrane, the seat of the Misses Cathcart, is perhaps the most charming spot on all "the banks and braes o' bonnie Doon." The bed of the river here is rocky, and the banks magnificently wooded. One is at a loss whether to admire most the natural beauty of the river, or the grand old monarchs of the forest, which stand along its banks. A walk through the grounds of this delightful residence is a treat not easily forgotten.

Minishant is a neat little village of about 100 inhabitants, famous for the manufacture of Scotch blankets. It is about 3½ miles from Maybole, on the low road to Ayr. Beside it stands an elegant church, erected by Sir Peter Coats as a memorial of Lady Coats. The church is non-sectarian, and is well-attended. Behind it is a Reading Room and Library—free to the people of the district. Close beside it is *Monkwood House*, and a little farther off is *Auchendrane* (Sir Peter Coats's), built on the site of the old castle of Auchendrane, the seat of the Mures, who came to an untimely end through participation in one of the old family feuds for which Carrick was conspicuous. Sir Walter Scott has dramatised the story in his poem of "Auchendrane, or the Ayrshire Tragedy." The grounds of Auchendrane are beautifully laid out; and in a rustic cottage there is to be seen a group of statuary representing the chief characters in Burns's poem of Tam o' Shanter. The mansion house is built in the old Scotch baronial style, and forms the handsomest residence in the parish. The Doon here begins to put on its mantle of beauty, which it never quits till it reaches the sea.

Dalmellington is about fifteen miles from Maybole. But if the visitor can spare the time, he should endeavour to see

Minishant Memorial Church.

the far-famed Loch Doon and its lonely castle; while he cannot fail being repaid by a walk down the Ness Glen, through which the river issues from the Loch. The Ness Glen, indeed, is the Queen of Ayrshire Glens; and the sight of those beetling "craigs," with the black oily-looking water rushing over the rocks below, while the whole pass is waving with foliage—is a vision which is "a joy for ever." Of it, much more truthfully than of the Falls of Moness, might Burns have written:

The braes ascend like lofty wa's,
The foamin' stream deep roarin' fa's,
O'erhung wi' fragrant spreadin' shaws,
The birks o' Aberfeldy.

Crosshill is three miles from Maybole. It was built for the hand-loom weaving trade, and is a prosaic enough looking village. In former days it was a centre of the Orange Societies; and in a field betwixt it and Maybole there occurred a tussle between them and the Yeomanry Cavalry (familiarly known as the "Sour Milk Jocks"), which was locally nicknamed the "Battle of Ballochbroe." The affair is thus briefly described in the *Ayr Advertiser* of date, July 13th, 1854:—"The twelfth of July passed off without any disturbance in Ayr. The usual Orange Ball was held in the evening. Four or five troops of the County Yeomanry Cavalry were called out to prevent any demonstrations at the places in the county where there was the most reason to apprehend outbreaks in consequence, such as Dalry, Kilbirnie, Dalmellington, Maybole, &c. The Orangemen of Maybole and Crosshill processed, despite the Sheriff's proclamation; but were stopped by Sheriff Robison and local magistrates at Maybole, and by Mr Dykes and Bailie Muir, Justices of the Peace, at Crosshill, assisted by the Yeomanry

Cavalry. The musical instruments and staves were taken from the parties; and at Crosshill, where the procession stoned the force employed in preserving the peace, one of the ringleaders was apprehended and sent to Ayr prison." This is all our local newspaper says about a riot which has been the nearest approach to a civil war the district has seen for many years.

NOTE.—In addition to the etymologies of our street names already given, the following may be interesting to some:—*Barns Terrace*, from a Public Barn which formerly stood in front of Barns house. *Society Row*, from the house in it built by the Maybole Benevolent Society in 1824. *Abbot Street*, from the fact that the Abbots of Crossraguel had their town residence here. *Inch's Closs*, from a former residenter who, for some reason or other, went under the name of "Inch about." *Mason Row* and *Smithy Brae* speak of the trades of those who lived in them. *Bullock Loaning* was the *Cowcaddens* of Maybole, and at one time formed the chief entrance into our town from the north. *Whitehall* was the name of a house which formerly stood near the Tolbooth, and probably near the site of the present *Spoon-creel*. *Dangartland* once belonged to the laird of Dangart in Colmonell parish. *The Path* tells of a time when public roads were unknown, and the *Heart Loch* describes its own peculiar outline. While *Lovers' Loaning* gives its own etymology, and forms one of an interesting family to be found in all towns!

OOR AIN BIT TOON.

A man may hae wandered to mony braw places,
But there's only ae place he can ca' his ain hame;
And that place is sacred—it's no like the ithers—
They may be far grander, but never the same.
For oor hame is the spot in this wilderness warld,
Whaur the life maun be leeved that 's to tak' us aboon;
It's the place in the Battle of life we've been posted,
To stan' for oor Master—oor ain bit toon.

We may look and may lang for some greater station, [display,
Whaur we think we could better our talents
But Here or Nowhere must we face what's assigned us,
Just Here or Nowhere must we carry the day.
Then let us tak' hold of the Task that's gi'en to us,
And let us work at it till life's en' comes roun',
And we'll yet thank the Father wha met us and bless'd us,
'Mang the hamely concerns o' oor ain bit toon.

CPSIA information can be obtained
at www.ICGtesting.com
Printed in the USA
LVHW051455271021
701703LV00011B/744

9 781166 930998